A Friend Indeed

June 1977

To Karen with much
affection and thanks.

Cecilia

A Friend Indeed

Warm Thoughts
On the Meaning of Friendship
Selected by Mary Alice Loberg
Illustrated by Arlene Noel

♛ Hallmark Editions

A Friend Indeed

y friends are

my estate.

Forgive me then

the avarice to hoard them!

Emily Dickinson

 friend is one to whom
one may pour out
all the contents of one's heart,
chaff and grain together,
knowing that
the gentlest of hands

will take and sift it,

    keep what is worth keeping,

and with a breath of kindness,

    blow the rest away.

Dinah Mulock Craik

ne of the very pleasant
things about friendship . . .
the do=you=remember moments.

Faith Baldwin

I want someone
        to laugh with me,
someone to be
        grave with me,
someone to please me

and help my discrimination
with his or her own remark,
and at times, no doubt,
to admire my acuteness
and penetration.

Robert Burns

Friendship

is in loving

rather than in being loved.

Robert Bridges

Friendship is the positive

and unalterable choice

of a person

whom we have singled out

for qualities

that we admire.

Abel Bonnard

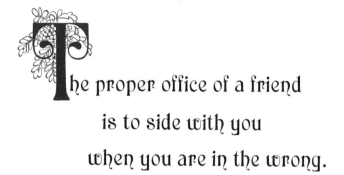

The proper office of a friend

is to side with you

when you are in the wrong.

Nearly anybody
will side with you
when you are right.

Mark Twain

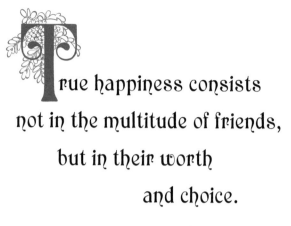

rue happiness consists
not in the multitude of friends,
but in their worth
and choice.

Ben Jonson

Friendship
that flows from the heart
cannot be frozen
by adversity,

as the water that flows

from the spring...

cannot congeal in winter.

James Fenimore Cooper

Friendship
is related to love,
and if love
is the bread of life,
friendship
is in the same package.

Gladys Taber

hatever else a friend
may be, she is never a bore
to her friend.
You like her because she is she
and you are you.

Jessamyn West

Once in an age,
God sends to some of us
a friend who loves in us
...not the man that we are,
but the angel we may be.

Harriet Beecher Stowe

riendship

has so much of Sovereignty,

yes and of Religion too,

that no prescription

can be admitted

against it.

John Donne

riendship

needs no words==

it is a loneliness

relieved of the anguish

of loneliness.

Dag Hammarskjold

rue friendship
foresees the needs of others
rather than proclaims its own.

André Maurois

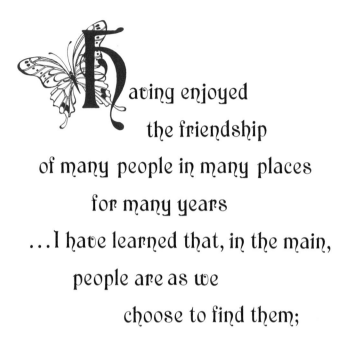

aving enjoyed
the friendship
of many people in many places
for many years
…I have learned that, in the main,
people are as we
choose to find them;

that reason

can overcome prejudice;

that knowledge

can overcome ignorance;

that love can overcome hate;

that goodness

can conquer evil.

Dore Schary

Your friend is your
needs answered.
He is your field which you sow
with love and reap with
thanksgiving. And he is
your board and your fireside.
For you come to him
with your hunger,
and you seek him for peace.

Kahlil Gibran